My New
Friend

By Jillian Powell

Photography by Chris Fairclough

Published in 2013 by Wayland
Copyright © Wayland 2013

Wayland
338 Euston Road
London NW1 3BH

Wayland Australia
Level 17/207 Kent Street
Sydney, NSW 2000

Editor, Wayland: Julia Adams
Produced for Wayland by Discovery Books Ltd
Managing editor: Rachel Tisdale
Project editor: Colleen Ruck
Designer: Ian Winton
Photography: Chris Fairclough
Consultant: Helen Beale (Teacher and Library Coordinator,
Robert Le Kyng Primary School, Swindon)

The author and photographer would like to acknowledge the
following for their help in preparing this book: Clementine, Adelina,
Haniya Lampkin-Berry, Mr and Mrs Lampkin-Berry; Emily, Megan,
Mr and Mrs Robinson; Headteacher Jane Johnson, staff and pupils
at Norton Primary School.

British Library Cataloguing in Publication Data
Powell, Jillian.
   My new friend.
   1. Friendship--Pictorial works--Juvenile literature.
   I. Title
   302.3'4-dc22

ISBN: 978 0 7502 7857 7

10 9 8 7 6 5 4 3 2 1

Printed in China

Wayland is a division of Hachette Children's Books, an Hachette UK company.
www.hachette.co.uk

Contents

my home

My name is Clementine. I live with my mum and dad and my two little sisters, Adelina and Haniya.

I share a bedroom with my little sister Adelina. We like to play together in our bedroom.

Neighbours

Emily and her family have just moved into a house down the road. I met Emily when we were both out on our bikes. She is my new **friend**.

I am **excited** because Emily is going to the same school as me. It is the first day back after the holidays.

Our mums walk to school with us.

Classmates

Emily is in the same class as me. Our class teacher, Miss Cundick, says we can sit next to each other. We write about what we did in the holidays.

After school, Mum comes to pick me up. She has been chatting to Emily's mum while she waited for me.

Visiting Emily

Emily has asked me to play at her house after school. Mum takes me there.

Emily says we can play in the garden.

Emily shows me
her dog, Poppy.
Poppy's fur feels
very soft. She is
really cute.

Playing together

Today Emily comes back to my house for tea. We have pizza with my sister Adelina.

After tea we play one
of my **favourite** games.

Emily has not played it before,
but she really enjoys it. We
both want to win!

Not friends?

In the playground at school today, Emily plays a clapping game with Sophie.

I want to join in, but Emily says I don't know the game.

When it is time for our PE lesson, Emily picks Sophie as her **partner**.

I feel sad because I don't think Emily wants to be my friend any more.

Together again

After school, Emily comes round to say she is sorry if she upset me. She still wants to be my friend.

It's nice to be friends again. Mum says it is okay to have lots of other friends, too.

Emily teaches me how to play the clapping game. It doesn't take me long to learn it!

Emily's birthday

It is Emily's birthday next week. I make a **friendship bracelet** for her.

I pick all her favourite colours.

I make a birthday card for Emily, too. I draw flowers on it because I know she likes them.

The party

Today is Emily's birthday and she is having a party. We all sit down for some party food.

Then I give Emily her friendship bracelet. She loves it. Emily says I am her best friend. She is my best friend, too!

Glossary

excited feeling happy and looking forward to something.

favourite something you like best of all.

friend someone you like to spend time with.

friendship bracelet a bracelet that you give to someone as a sign of friendship.

partner someone you pair up with.

Further information

Books

Thoughts and Feelings: Making Friends by Sarah Levete (Franklin Watts, 2007)

Healthy and Happy: Family and Friends by Louise Spilsbury (Wayland, 2009)

A First Look At: Respect For Others – Everybody Matters by Pat Thomas (Wayland, 2010)

Websites

www.bbc.co.uk/cbbc/bugbears
An interactive website that provides advice about friends and friendships.

www.cyh.com
The Kids' Health section of this website includes helpful facts and information about topics such as making friends and friendships.

www.kidshealth.org/kid/feeling
This website includes practical information about dealing with thoughts and feelings such as feeling shy.

Things to do

Literacy/Speaking and Listening
Write down two single words that best describe your new friend. You can discuss your choices with your friend and the rest of your class.

Art
Make a collage of pictures of your friend's favourite things. Cut out lots of different pictures from newspapers and magazines and stick them onto coloured card. Your friend will love it!

Index